Spiritual Warfare

for

Lost Loved Ones

FRANK HAMMOND

SPIRITUAL WARFARE FOR LOST LOVED ONES

BY FRANK HAMMOND

ISBN 10: 0-89228-384-X
ISBN 13: 978-089228-384-2

IMPACT CHRISTIAN BOOKS, INC.
332 Leffingwell Ave., Suite 101
Kirkwood, MO 63122

WWW.IMPACTCHRISTIANBOOKS.COM

All scripture quotations are from the King James Version of the Bible unless otherwise noted.

Scripture quotations identified NASB are from the New American Standard Bible® (NASB), Copyright © 1960, 1962, 1963, 1968, 1971, 1972, 1973, 1975, 1977, 1995 by The Lockman Foundation. Used by permission. www.Lockman.org.

For a full list of Impact's titles, refer to the website above or use your camera with the **QR Code**

INTRODUCTION

People often ask us as we travel to minister, "What can we do about family members? What can we do about friends and loved ones who are lost, or living a life of sin and taken over by the devil?" This question concerns the people in your life who are outside the family of God, but who do not want any help. They are simply not open for direct ministry.

Now, maybe we ask that question out of our own frustration. For instance, "Lord, if you deal with them, it will be easier for me!" We all have done this at some point, it is part of being human.

However, most come to me out of a genuine concern for lost loved ones. They know that Satan is working in the lives of the lost, and they don't want to see other people's lives destroyed, especially those close to them. "We don't want to see them in misery; we don't want to see them tormented and oppressed by the devil. Is there anything that we can do to help people like that?" they ask.

This is what we're going to be talking about in the following pages. What can we do about people we love, our friends and our close family members, who are not open to direct help? What can do?

DETERMINING THE SPIRITUAL NEED

One of the first steps we need to take is to determine where the person really is spiritually, and by that I mean, define where they are in their own personal relationship with the Lord Jesus Christ. Has he or she ever been born again? Are they a child of God?

Let's look at this verse in 2 Corinthians 4:3–4,

But if our gospel be hid, it is hid to them that are lost: in whom the god of this world hath blinded the minds of them which believe not, lest the light of the glorious gospel of Christ, who is the image of God, should shine unto them.

Some people simply do not know the Gospel. They have not been able to receive salvation because they are blinded.

Notice the word "god of this world" is not capitalized; it is not referring to Jehovah, the Lord God, but rather to Satan. Satan is the god of this world, for now. As such, anyone following the world is following Satan, because he is the god of this world. The course of this world is being set by Satan. So if some of our friends and loved ones are following in the ways of the world, and they are walking in the paths of sin, they are not walking in the wisdom of God; they are not walking in the truth of God. The reason for that is that Satan is the god of this world,

Do you have lost loved ones who have a chip on their shoulder towards God? Who say, "Don't talk to me about God, don't bring that Bible out while I'm around, don't quote that Scripture to me!" What makes people act like that? They are blinded; they are deceived. Satan has cut them off from their true spiritual resource. They get uncomfortable around you because you are walking in the Spirit and you are walking in the ways of God, and that makes them uncomfortable. By nature of you being in their lives, and having the Lord's presence in you, you are bringing life and light into their life. That light makes those evil spirits in them restless; it makes those spirits cringe and recoil.

So we need to understand what's going on, because often when we get upset with the person, it's not their flesh that is the cause. We need to be able to love the person and see beyond that disturbance in their life, and know what is causing that disturbance. Paul says it this way:

For is not against flesh and blood…

Eph. 6:12, NASB

The way forward then is to attack the enemy that stirred up these reactions in that person rather than attack the person himself.

BLINDED BY A DEMON?

Is there anything that we can do about a person who is blinded by the devil? Did you know that we have the power through Jesus to bind the ruler spirit (strongman) over lost loved ones? We need to come into spiritual battle against the enemy, the demons, that blind our friends and our loved ones from being able to receive the truth and Scripture, from being able to pray, or open up their hearts to receive the things of God. Receiving the things of God is what is going to set them free.

They can't get set free without God and the Word of God. So if a demon is keeping them blinded, then we can go to battle against that demon and say, "you are bound, enemy! You spirit that comes against my family, that comes against my loved ones, we bind you in the name of Jesus!"

We have known people who were bound by Satan and lost to Jesus. When those demons were bound, a veil was lifted off of them and they were able to see and respond!

There was a fellow in our church who recently came to the Lord. He had been so obstinate and combative toward the Lord for years. His wife had married him while he was in this state and had become unequally yoked together with him, as he was not a believer at the time. She was out of the will of God. When you marry out of the will of God and become unequally yoked with an unbeliever then you have to call on the mercy of God to intervene: "Lord I made a mistake and I didn't follow your counsel, please save my husband/wife!" That's what this woman did.

As well, our church prayed for that man for several years. He was a drug addict, and he drank a lot, among other things.

Do you know what happened? That husband got saved a few months ago and now he is a regular in church, both he and his wife and their little baby. Now he is walking in the ways of God! The wife waited through years of real pressure in her life because her husband didn't know the Lord. Through binding that strongman and continuing to bring that light and truth to this man, eventually he came to a saving knowledge of the Lord Jesus Christ.

WORK OUT YOUR SALVATION

Philippians 2:12–13 says,

> … **work out your own salvation with fear and trembling.**
> **For it is God which worketh in you…**

What does this mean? When a person gets saved, he or she has a responsibility to work out his or her salvation. Sometimes we have family members or loved ones who have been born again and they are really children of God but they are not working out their own salvation. There are demonic spirits hindering them and seeking to prevent them from growing spiritually and getting their life in order in the Lord.

It says here to "work out your own salvation." We can't do that for our loved ones. Eventually, they have to cooperate with God on their own.

Nonetheless, there are some things that we can do about those who are not working out their salvation.

THREE STRATEGIC STEPS WE MUST TAKE

God has shown us three very basic things that we need to keep in the forefront of our spirit as we deal with these people that we want to see come to the Lord. The first thing is that we need to be continually in prayer, in *intercessory prayer.* Ephesians 6:18 lists seven pieces of spiritual armor that are given to us by which to fight Satan and overcome his wiles. The seventh piece, the last piece, the capstone piece, is prayer:

> **Praying always with all prayer and supplication in the Spirit… for all the saints.**

Dear reader, prayer is a powerful weapon. Do not underestimate intercessory prayer. It is a defensive weapon and an offensive weapon. You see, prayer is protection for us such that when we are in prayer we are protecting ourselves. But also, through prayer, we can help protect others who may not be vigilant to protect themselves.

There are a lot of people who are not interested in protecting themselves, at this stage in their life. God puts those people on our hearts, does He not? We are involved in their lives so that we can know when we need to pray and intercede for them. This kind of prayer is like putting an umbrella over them. We put a spiritual umbrella over them to protect them when they are not interested enough to protect themselves. We protect them in that interim period while we are waiting for them to come to their own decision of will, to come to their own convictions, to come to their own relationship with the Lord, and begin to stand in their own battles. We "hold the umbrella" while they begin to discipline their own lives, and begin to receive the truth of God, which is what really sets them free. So intercessory prayer is a tremendous weapon that the Lord has given to us.

When we are in intercessory prayer, remember that you have to pray in faith. In James 1, we are reminded that if we do not pray in faith we cannot expect to receive anything from the Lord. Sometimes the situations that we face in our relationship with others look dark. They look pretty hopeless, don't they? If we begin to waver and doubt at any point along the way then we are decreasing our chances of getting the victory in that situation. When you are without faith, you cannot expect your intercessory prayer to avail anything. Scripture says that when we ask, we must ask in faith, not wavering. According to James 1:6-7, he that wavers is

> **"For he that wavereth is like a wave of the sea driven with the wind and tossed. For let not that man think that he shall receive any thing of the Lord."**

We are going to have to be strong in our faith, and we are going to have to believe God. We are going to have to anchor ourselves in the Word of God when we come to pray for our loved ones.

The second thing that we need to be involved in is *spiritual warfare*. Technically, there is a difference between prayer and spiritual warfare, although they are very closely related and intermingled. Most of the time when I'm in spiritual warfare it is interlaced with prayers and intercessions; it is a back and forth process, woven like fabric together. But the basic difference is that prayer is addressed to God; when we're praying we are talking to God. When we are in spiritual warfare, we are talking to the devil. Not only do we pray to God and intercede and ask for God's mercy in the working of God's Spirit in a situation, but also we enter into direct confrontation with the enemy. The Holy Spirit will lead you in this.

We must realize that we cannot control another person's will. Trying to control another person's will is opposite to the goal of deliverance and spiritual warfare, and is tantamount to *witchcraft*. Instead, spiritual warfare has as its goal the releasing of a person's will in order that he can respond directly to the Lord and receive the help God has for him. There is a freedom that often comes into someone's life through this form of spiritual warfare. Binding the devil in this situation may not cause a person to turn. However, binding the work of the enemy in that life provides a freer atmosphere for change, and the best chance for that person to choose Christ and His kingdom!

We do this in the anointing of God's Holy Spirit, not off the top of our heads. We need to let the Holy Spirit, who is in us, lead the battle. We need to let Him show us the specific demons that are in a person that need to be bound; the spirits that are preventing this person from coming to the Lord. Maybe, for instance, it is the spirit of rebellion and you need to first bind that rebellious spirit. In other situations, it could be the spirit of pride and this demon is keeping a person from coming to know the Lord, and acknowledging his sins and confessing his mistakes.

I talked to someone the other day about a certain man, and I said "what he needs to do is to come to repentance." This man, who'd been witnessing to him, said, "I don't think he knows how to repent." Well, I thought about that for a minute. Repentance is not that complicated, it means to simply turn around from the direction that you are going and head in the opposite direction. It means to turn away from your path of sin and from chasing after the ways of the devil, and receive God's forgiveness and God's help. There is nothing complicated about forgiveness and repentance, except that the devil tries to block people from turning around. Demons make people puffed up with pride and settled in the rebellion that comes into their hearts; those are two of the main things that stand in the road when a person needs to repent before the Lord and get things right between himself and God.

So we need to come into spiritual warfare and bind those powers. Remember the lesson that Jesus gave us in Matthew 12, where He set the priority that we must *first bind the strong man and then we can spoil his house.* In these kinds of situations, we want to spoil the devil's house, meaning we are going to take away a captive that he holds! We must bind the strongman that holds that person in bondage.

The third thing that we need to remember, as we come into a desire to see our loved ones and friends set free, is the **ministry of love.** Love is such a powerful ministry. We know from long-standing experience that practically every person who has an upheaval in his personality, a person that is captured by the devil, most likely feels that few, if any, love him.

If you would stop for a moment, and notice this, it would help a great deal in your ministry to that person. One of the main things that person needs is love. That is something that all of us have, right? Love is not submission to the sin or addictions of the lost loved one. Rather it is a consistent expression of where the Lord's heart is for this person. If you have love, you can give it.

The devil tries to block your gift of love. He will tell you that the lost one doesn't deserve any love. He will try to keep us cut off from the flow of love and from giving love because the devil knows that love is going to do more to heal that person and bring them to the Lord than anything else you can do! The devil hates love.

So we have to release that love. If we let resentment, frustration and impatience build up, these things cut off that flow of love. The flow of love has to be there in order for the healing to come forth.

We are anticipating, praying, interceding, and believing for this person to turn back to righteousness; to repent and come back to the Lord. Now if you have loved that person, if you have not attacked that person and assaulted them because of the problems that they created in your own life, you have left a very important door open. If they know that you have loved them despite all of their ornery ways, and all the hurts and abuses that they may be responsible for toward you, if you have continued to forgive them — and forgiveness is an expression of love —

then when that day comes when they want to come back to the Lord, they will have an opening to come to you because you haven't shut them off. You have continued to love them.

In your own life they can see an example of God's forgiveness. Some people who have been in rebellion and lived in sin get hopeless and think "Well, I might as well just live in this condition forever because there's no way back. I'm sure God will not forgive me after all I've done." That is one of the big lies the devil tells people; "You have blown it. You have gone too far. After all you've done you could never be received back in God's family." They don't understand the principle that is in the parable of the prodigal son. It is the principle of a love that never gives up.

If they see forgiveness in us, then what they see is a manifestation of God's propensity to forgive them. If they can see that example, then it will help them to understand the forgiveness and the mercy of God. No matter where they have been, no matter what they've done, God's love is great enough to reach out and minister to them, save them and deliver them.

Now, the person must eventually come back into his own relationship with the Lord. He must eventually repent of his sins; he must receive the truth of the Lord Jesus which is going to set him free. But he needs help before he gets to that point, and that is what God wants to use me and you to do.

KEEP OUR HEARTS IN CHECK

Often there are situations that arise where we become a part of the problem. Right? We get drawn in and we start doing a lot of things where our actions are not Christian. Somebody around us is not acting like a Christian and they're not showing us love or kindness, and we are tempted to react to their actions. But if we react in a wrong way, we are as guilty of sin as they are. If we get mad, then we have sinned. If we get frustrated, or impatient, or depressed and hopeless because of that situation, then we have sinned and we need to find our own way back in relationship to God. We need to do this because we have to be strong for the person we are praying for, who is weak. It is just that simple.

I'm sure, as we begin to talk about these things, that most of you have people within your own family you are praying for. Maybe it's your spouse. Men, perhaps it's your wife. For you wives, it may be your husbands. For you parents, it might be your children. For children, it might be their parents. Or, perhaps, your uncle, your grandpa and grandma, or your mother-in-law. But there's somebody that you are burdened about today. There's somebody that needs to come into the ways the Lord. Satan has a hook in their nose and is leading them around, and you want to know what in the world you can do about it.

THE EXAMPLE OF NEHEMIAH

I want you to know this morning that I am ministering to you out of a heart of concern and understanding. We have had a situation like this in our family. Our family has been in one of the most intense, spiritual battles and intercessory prayer situations that we've ever seen. We have won some victories, but we haven't seen the full measure of victory that we hoped to see when we first started into this situation. But we can't quit. We have to press on.

I would like to share some things from experience with you.

When you get in these battles, let the Lord direct you in your prayer and your warfare, through his Word. His Word is the most solid ground that you can get on. God gave us very specific scriptures, a lot of them out of Psalms, and some in Isaiah. Throughout the Scriptures the Lord has guided us in these things to give us insight as to where we are in this battle and what we are to do on certain days, in certain situations and at certain times.

I am not trying to give you just one specific Scripture for you to use for yourself. I don't want you to get lazy in the word of God. I want you to know that the word of God, and the prayers of fellow saints, is what is going to direct you. God will probably give you some personalized picture that is going to be pertinent to you in your situation. But of all the verses we have received from the Lord, this one that follows is a good one!

In Nehemiah 4:14 we read:

> **And I looked, and rose up, and said unto the nobles, and to the rulers, and to the rest of the people, Be not ye afraid of them**...

Nehemiah is telling the people to not be afraid of their enemies. Nehemiah had gone back from Babylon to rebuild the walls of Jerusalem that had been torn down when God's judgment came upon that people. And now the enemy is harassing them and trying to prevent that wall from being rebuilt.

> **Be not ye afraid of them: remember the LORD, which is great and terrible, and fight for your brethren, your sons, and your daughters, your wives, and your houses. [i.e. your households].**
>
> Neh. 4:14

Everyone that lives in your household, everyone that is a part of your family, the Word of God says to "fight for them!" Fight for your "brethren, your sons and your daughters, your wives and your households." Through this, God says to us today:

"Remember that the Lord Christ is with you. The Lord is strong; the Lord is mighty; He is the Lord of hosts, the Lord of armies. He will fight on your behalf. Get in the battle and don't let your family go down without resistance. Put up resistance and fight for your family!"

NEHEMIAH'S ENEMY IS A TYPE OF SATAN

Going back to Nehemiah 4:1,

> **But it came to pass, that when Sanballat heard that we builded the wall, he was wroth, and took great indignation, and mocked the Jews.**
>
> Neh. 4:1

When the Jews came back, Sanballat was one of those rulers who lived nearby to Jerusalem. He enjoyed the fact that Jerusalem had been destroyed and that for 70 years the place had been in desolation. He also enjoyed ready access into and out of Jerusalem, because the wall was torn down. His pleasure came from the desperate plight of God's people.

Sometimes we can learn a great deal about a situation in Scripture by examining the names of the men involved. These names can often be prophetic, and they open up and give us revelation and understanding. In this case, the name Sanballat literally means "a fallen branch." So here was a man described by the Lord as a "fallen branch." Do you know anybody else that has fallen, that Sanballat might represent? Satan is the one who fell. Jesus said, "I beheld Satan as lightning fall from heaven."

Satan was a glorious one at one time. There is a lot of evidence that he was perhaps one of God's choice archangels and that he occupied a very important place in the ranks of heaven. But he was lifted up in his pride, and he thought to exalt himself even above the throne of God, and he fell. He had to be cast out of heaven. So Sanballat is a type or prophetic image of the devil. He represents "the fallen one."

Sanballat became exceedingly angry when he saw that the wall of Jerusalem was being rebuilt! Why did that upset Sanballat so much? It meant that when that wall was built he could not get back into Jerusalem. A wall is built for protection, it exists as a hedge. In Old Testament days the cities all sought to have walls around them because that was their protection. As long as they had the wall, they had a defense against the enemy.

Can you see that is what is supposed to take place in your life and in my life? We ought to have spiritual walls built up in our lives. So long as we have those spiritual walls in our lives, then the enemy is not going to be able to get through to us. He is stopped outside the walls and cannot harass us from within.

Take a quick look in Proverbs 25:28:

He that hath no rule over his own spirit is like a city that is broken down and without walls.

The man who is not disciplined in his spiritual life does not have his guard up. Proverbs compares him to a city whose walls are broken down. The city that has the walls broken down is a city that is vulnerable to attack. That is precisely what has happened to some of our loved ones; their walls are broken down! As long as their walls are broken down then there is vulnerability.

God spoke to the prophet Isaiah and He said, essentially, "I was surprised that there was no intercessor there, no one to stand in the gap." So their walls were broken down and there was no one to step in to fill that gap until that wall could be rebuilt.

That is the position that God wants you and me to fill in relationship to others. When their wall is torn down, we need to stand in the gap, and help edify them. Did you know that the word edify means to "build up"? Our ministry to lost loved ones is to build. If we're frustrated or defeated or depressed or hopeless, there is no way that we can help in that situation until we get our heart right, and we can no longer be a factor in helping that person rebuild their wall. We need to stand in the gap and at the same time be busy with rebuilding the wall.

THE MOCKERY OF SATAN

So Nehemiah was facing this situation with Sanballat. When he heard the wall had been built, Sanballat…

took great indignation, and mocked the Jews.

Mockery is one of the weapons that Satan uses against us. That was one of the things that he used against Jesus. All the way through the crucifixion experience of Jesus there was mockery. When he hung on the cross, those before Him said mockingly, "You said you were the king of the Jews. You said that you save others, let's see you save yourself." The enemy was trying to destroy through mockery and to damage faith and confidence.

Have you ever heard Satan talk like that to you? Saying "It's just not going to work. It just can't be done. This thing is impossible, you might as well quit. You might as well give up." So that is what the devil does, he comes alongside to mock you. He says "You are supposed to be a Christian! You are supposed to have spiritual authority! Well, look at the situation, it's not getting better, it's getting worse!" You have been praying and you have been seeking God, but things are more desperate now than they ever have been. So the enemy has a chance to come in and to ridicule and mock and despise us.

Are we going to let him get away with that? Are we going to listen to all those ugly things he has to say, that God doesn't have any power or that the ways of God don't work? That we might as well lie down and give up in defeat because what we have believed is just not paying off? That is exactly where Satan wants us, in that "give up" attitude.

Sanballat questions the resolve of God's people:

> **And he spake before his brethren and the army of Samaria, and said, What do these feeble Jews? will they fortify themselves? will they sacrifice? will they make an end in a day? will they revive the stones out of the heaps of the rubbish which are burned?**
>
> Neh. 4:2

Sanballat has an army, just like Satan has an army. Again, he is a type of Satan. So he said to his demonically-inspired army, "These Jews are trying to get that wall rebuilt and if they do it, we are not going to be able to move in and out of those people's lives like we have in the past, so we have to do something." So he began to call his whole army together. Do you get the picture? Satan sees when you are trying to get that wall rebuilt. He is not going to give up without a battle. He tries to resist the wall-building efforts.

However, we can become so aware of what the devil is doing, that our focus is taken off what Jesus is doing. One of the things God is doing in these last days is to open our eyes so that we can see what we are doing to the devil! Rather than wringing our hands and worrying what the devil is doing to us, we are being encouraged about the power of our prayer and intercession and its effect on the camp of the enemy. Amen! When God lifts the curtain and lets us look at the realm of Satan's headquarters where he sets up all his plans and works all his devices, then we begin to see what we are doing to the devil. We need to see that.

We see the devil in this instance, represented by Sanballat, and he is giving himself a pep-talk. He is trying to build himself up. He is saying, "These Jews are not going to succeed." Like he says today, "these Christians are not going to succeed." And "their spiritual weapons are not going to avail anything."

Sanballat said,

> **What do these feeble Jews? will they fortify themselves? will they sacrifice? will they make an end in a day? will they revive the stones out of the heaps of the rubbish which are burned?**
>
> Neh. 4:2

He called them "feeble Jews," not because they were feeble but because he wanted to believe they were feeble. In reality, they were God's children; they were the heirs of the promises of God. They had God on their side!

Who are we? Do you know who you are? Are you a weak Christian? That is really a paradox – there is no such thing as a weak Christian. You can't be anything but strong because it's the same Spirit that lives in you that raised Jesus from the dead. The power of resurrection life is in you by the indwelling presence of God's Holy Spirit. The Lord Jesus said not that we are conquerors, but that we are more than conquerors. We are *overcomers*! We can do all things through Christ who strengthens us.

Yet the devil wants to come along and say "what are these feeble Jews going to do?" Or in our terms, "what are these feeble Christian going to do?" He is trying to convince himself so that he can convince us that we are feeble and weak.

Do you remember when the children of Israel came out of Egypt, and they went through experiences at Mount Sinai where God gave them the law? Then it was time for them to go into Canaan. You see, God never intended for them to live in the wilderness for 40 years, or for a whole generation of them to die in the wilderness. No, he intended for them to cross the Jordan and go in. But they sent the spies out. They sent 12 spies and 10 of those 12 spies came back and said "we're nothing but feeble Jews!" They said, "why over yonder there are giants and walled cities, and we are just like grasshoppers in their sight!" They saw themselves as weak, as feeble, as mere grasshoppers in the presence of those giants. What could they do? They believed they could not do anything. That is the reason they died in the wilderness; that's the reason a whole generation of them died in the wilderness. That is the reason that they didn't enter into the promises of God, because they saw themselves as feeble rather than seeing themselves as strong in the Lord! The Lord had brought them through the plagues in Egypt. He had opened up the Red Sea. He had fed them supernaturally. He had manifested His presence in glory and power with thunder and lightening and voices on Mt. Sinai and then they said "We can't do it."

This is where some of us are today. We are not feeble. We are quite the opposite!

Sanballat goes on to ask another question:

"will they fortify themselves?"

He said, "do they think that they're going to do this by themselves without any help?" He is trying to convince himself that these Jews don't have anybody to help them. And, today, he tries to convince us that we do not have anyone to help us. Are we going to do these things by ourselves? Are we going to be able to accomplish all of these things and restore all of this without any assistance?

But we do have assistance. We have the help of the Lord of armies!

Sometimes the problems that we have are because of sin. The problem that the children of Israel had in the wilderness was because of their sin. The problem that Nehemiah and his people had was because of sin. That is the reason they went off into captivity and the reason the judgment of God came upon Jerusalem. That is the reason the walls were torn down. It was because of sin. And the enemy comes along and says in our ear, "Yes. You are just reaping what you sowed. You are going to have to live with this; there is nothing you can do about it. You made your bed for yourself and you are going to have to lie in it the rest of your life."

But one thing the enemy had not reckoned with was the grace of God. Where sin abounds, grace abounds much more. It super abounds!

Satan also forgets that God is in the restoring business. He is a restorer of lives, and of protective walls around those lives. If God wasn't in this business, all of us would have all been stamped out a long time ago. If we received what we deserved, we would all be in bad shape. But the thing about God's grace is that He provides things that we don't deserve. Hallelujah! There is deliverance in Zion, not because we deserve it but because God loves us and His grace is poured on us!

Sanballat asks another question:

"will they sacrifice?"

The temple had been torn down and the Jews could not offer sacrifices. This meant they had been cut off from God. They had no relationship with God as a people because of these circumstances.

Sanballat asked, "Are the sacrifices going to be restored?" You see, the sacrifices he was referring to were like the sacrifice of Jesus. All those animal sacrifices were fulfilled when Jesus Christ died on the cross. So the sacrifices speak of all of the redemptive benefits that are in the Lord Jesus Christ. The devil is asking the question to himself about us, saying "Are those people going to get back into the things of God? Are they really going to be restored in their spiritual worship? As they really going to be restored into praise? Are they going to be restored in the truth? Are they going to be walking in the power of God's Holy Spirit? Are all of these spiritual blessings going to be restored?"

You see how nervous the devil is when God's people begin to get serious about the things of God?

He says,

> **"Will they make an end in a day?"**

That devil had been sitting atop that heap of stones for 70 years. Everything had been going his way. He saw the Jews coming back and putting the stones back in place and building that wall, and he said, "What do they think they are going to do? Why, I took 70 years to get this place torn down, and do they think they can build it back in such a short amount of time?"

Here is part of the miracle in this story, and in your intercession for your loved ones. Do you know how long it took to rebuild the walls of Jerusalem — a monumental task? 52 days! That is what it took to rebuild that wall. So you can see why the enemy is so afraid today. He was thinking, "You mean, these families are going to be restored and it is going to be in such a short amount of time?"

Sanballat goes on and says,

> **"will they revive the stones out of the heaps of the rubbish which are burned?"**

He said "These stones are burnt! They are in bad condition! What can you do with these old burnt stones?" Apparently when you burn a stone it becomes weaker and sometimes crumbles. It loses a lot of its strength.

At this point some of the Jews began to get a little weak.

> **And Judah said, The strength of the bearers of burdens is decayed, and there is much rubbish; so that we are not able to build the wall.**
>
> Neh. 4:10

Judah wanted to give up. Do you know what Judah means? The name Judah means "praise." Nehemiah is talking about all the people of Judah here. They became discouraged, and they begin to doubt. And the first thing they lost was *praise!* This is one of the ways we know when the devil is beginning to get victory in our life is when we are not able to praise the Lord, not only at church but also at home.

Sometimes we can put up a front at church, and pretend that we are really free in our spirit. But I want to know, can you praise at home? Can you get your hands in the air, can you glorify the Lord, can you dance unto the Lord? If you cannot, then you know the devil is getting in his licks.

> **Now Tobiah the Ammonite was by him, and he said, Even that which they build, if a fox go up, he shall even break down their stone wall.**
>
> Neh. 4:3

Sanballat has a helper! This is like the prince spirit that Satan sends, the strongman, against our families. Do you know what the name Tobiah means? This is an interesting one. The name Tobiah means "God is good." So Satan sends this prince spirit as a co-worker and his name says "God is good." This is an old term of mockery; Tobiah is a spirit of mockery.

The mocker says: "Why you Jews have been believing that God is a good God. If God is so good, then why hasn't He done something? If God is so good, then why has He left this thing so desolate for so long?"

This is more ridicule and intimidation. This old mocker whose name means "God is good," comes along and says, "Well, even if they rebuild this wall, it will be so weak that if a little fox jumps up against that wall it will come tumbling down." We learn that the little foxes can "spoil the vines," in the Song of Solomon. What he is saying is, "Sanballat, we don't have to send all our army against this thing. Just send a few little spirits, just a few little foxes can knock that wall down."

Jesus talked about the devil being like "serpents and scorpions," and He said, "I give you power to tread on serpents and scorpions." I see people that run away from serpents, who run away from scorpions. They run away from little bugs. But in the spiritual realm we must not be cowards like that. Because the Lord has said, "I have given you power to tread upon them. You can step on them and kill them and stomp the life out of them." Glory to God!

KNOWING THE ENEMY'S PLANS

Everything that Sanballat and Tobiah were saying is written into Scripture. How did the writers of Scripture know about those things? How did Nehemiah know about the things that were going on in the private counsel of the enemy? Because God revealed it to him.

Do you remember the story from the life of Elisha the prophet? The enemy king had come against Israel. God would speak to Elisha and then Elisha would warn the king of Israel and tell him what the enemy king was plotting. Elisha would say to the king of Israel, "the enemy has brought his troops to a certain place over there, in that valley, behind that hill. So you avoid that place." This kept happening: the enemy king would try a maneuver and surprise the Israelites, and every time the camp of Israel knew exactly what the enemy was doing! And so the enemy king was disturbed and held a conference with his own leaders, and he said

"There is a betrayer in our midst!" He thought somebody was a spy for those Israelites, because they knew every move the enemy was making. Then one of his advisors spoke up and told the king it was not anyone in his counsel, but it was the prophet. He said "God is telling that prophet everything you privately say in your bedchamber."

We need to take heart with that! We need to understand that! When we are walking in the ways of God, there is no need for us to walk in ignorance about the devices of the devil. God wants us to know what the devil is doing and if we seek the Lord and pray, God will show us everything that the enemy is planning.

It's been amazing to us that through these our trials as we have sought the Lord, we have never had to walk in darkness; we have never walked away from the knowledge of what is happening. God has shown us step-by-step, day-by-day, circumstance-by-circumstance where the devil is in this situation and what he's been doing against us. It is good to know what is going on in the secret counsel of the enemy.

In verses 4 and 5, Nehemiah began to pray. Read what might be considered a strange prayer:

> **Hear, O our God; for we are despised: and turn their reproach upon their own head, and give them for a prey in the land of captivity:**
>
> **And cover not their iniquity, and let not their sin be blotted out from before thee: for they have provoked thee to anger before the builders.**

What the Lord revealed to me here was that Nehemiah was including God in that word "we;" he is not just talking about "we people" or "we Jews" but he said that we, including God, are despised. You see an attack against God's people is an attack against God! An attack against your family is an attack against you.

POUR IT ON THEM, LORD!

The core meaning of this prayer by Nehemiah is, "Lord, pour it on them!" He is asking God to deal harshly with his spiritual enemy! Scripture says that we don't have to love the devil. We have to hate those who hate God. That's our position. We don't have any mercy toward him or his demons.

Essentially, what Nehemiah is praying is for all the plans that the enemy has drawn up to be thrown into confusion. The psalmist prayed similarly, that his enemies would be thrown into confusion. Turn to Psalm 79, and I will give you one example where the psalmist prays like this:

O remember not against us former iniquities (v. 8)

The psalmist reminds us that we are not a prisoner of our past. God will forgive us of our past sins.

> **...let thy tender mercies speedily prevent us: for we are brought very low. Help us, O God of our salvation, for the glory of thy name: and deliver us, and purge away our sins, for thy name's sake.**
>
> **Wherefore should the heathen [i.e. the enemy] say, Where is their God?**

He is saying "Don't let the enemy taunt us and mock us."

> **...let him be known among the heathen in our sight by the revenging of the blood of thy servants which is shed.**
>
> **Let the sighing of the prisoner come before thee; according to the greatness of thy power preserve thou those that are appointed to die;**

And render unto our neighbours sevenfold into their bosom their reproach, wherewith they have reproached thee, O Lord.

So we thy people and sheep of thy pasture will give thee thanks for ever: we will shew forth thy praise to all generations.

The Psalmist prayed, "Lord, give our enemies seven times as bad as they have given us." We need to pray for those spiritual enemies to be confused and frustrated in the work of the devil. That is the way that God has taught us to pray.

THE DEVIL OVERPLAYS HIS HAND

Notice that Nehemiah did not get upset, but just calmly prayed and declared:

"God, you are still in charge. You are still on your throne. You see what the enemy has done. Lord just let him overplay his hand. Just let him get himself into such a big mess that he is going to end up in seven times more trouble than he started out with."

Often the devil starts out thinking he is going to get away with something and then he doesn't. When Jesus was crucified, Satan was the one who crucified Him, according to Paul. So every one of the events and all the circumstances in the crucifixion, including what Judas did, the denial by Peter with the desertion by the other disciples, and all the cruel abuses — all of that was the working of Satan. When Satan saw Jesus on the cross taking His last breath, he said "Ha! I have won!" There are times where it may look like the devil has won. It is when we get to the end of the rope that we say, "the devil has won!" But God was not through.

Scripture says that had Satan known that Jesus was going to rise again from the dead, he never would crucified Him!

I was pastoring a church many years ago and there was a little five-year-old boy in the fellowship. He moved in the spirit, that little boy. He had visions, and did not even know how to pronounce the word: he called it a "bision" like with a "b." One day he told his mother and dad that he had a "bision." They asked, "What did you see?" And he said, "Well I saw a rock, and this rock was going down a road. It was walking down this road. And then," he said, "there was a snake that chased the rock. And it caught the rock and he carried it off to his hole." And he looked puzzled and asked his dad, "Do snakes have holes?" He was just reporting what he had seen. And he said, "This snake took this rock into the hole, but it could not keep the rock in the hole. The rock came out and began to go down the road again and when the serpent started to chase Him again, a boomerang fell on him and killed the snake!" He said, "Daddy, what is a boomerang?"

This five-year-old boy had a revelation and he needed help to understand what he had seen. Jesus is the Rock. He is going through life and through his earthly ministry. Satan, the serpent, comes after him, seeks to capture him and take him in to his hole, into the grave. But he can't hold Jesus in death; he can't hold Jesus in the tomb. And so Jesus comes out and the boomerang falls on the devil. Hallelujah!

Glory to God! Thank you Jesus for that. Oh for the delivering power of the Lord Jesus Christ. Amen!

Some of you today think Satan has won. Don't give up! Don't quit! Continue to believe God. God still has a boomerang!

The things that look so defeated can be reversed. We must hold on in our faith and in our belief. What should we do then? Build the wall.

So built we the wall   Neh. 4:6

See, that is the objective. The purpose is to rebuild the wall.

INSIGHT FROM JUDE

Let's take another side trip from Nehemiah and look in the book of Jude for additional insight.

> **These be they who separate themselves, sensual, having not the Spirit.**
>
> **Jude 19**

Or a more literal translation would be, "These be they who cause divisions."

Do you have anybody in your family or your circle of acquaintances who causes divisions? I am sure you do. Jude tells you why they cause divisions: "they are sensual, having not the Spirit." They are not walking after the Spirit, they are walking after their own sensual appetites and their own sensual desires. They are walking after their own minds and the lusts of their own bodies. Jude says because they are not walking by the Spirit, they are causing separation, they are causing division.

Some of you are living in situations where division and separation have occurred because others around you are not walking in the Spirit but they're walking sensually.

> **But ye, beloved, building up yourselves on your most holy faith, praying in the Holy Ghost,....**
>
> **Jude 20**

He says saints, while this is going on don't you become part of the problem. Don't you aggregate the problem. Don't you be responsible for division and strife. Instead of that, keep building yourself up in the most holy things, praying in the Holy Ghost. Do you know how you pray in the

Holy Ghost? You pray in tongues. When you pray in tongues, Scripture says, "he that prays in an unknown tongue edifies himself." He builds himself up. When we build ourselves up we become stronger in faith.

Keep yourselves in the love of God, looking for the mercy of our Lord Jesus Christ unto eternal life.

Jude 21

Keep yourselves in the love of God. When others around us are acting negative and mean, it is easy to get resentful; it is easy to hate. It is easy to open the door where unforgiveness gets into our hearts. It is easy for the spirit of retaliation to rise up in us, that spirit that says, "You deserve to get even. You have some rights yourself." He said we had better keep ourselves in the love of God. This word "keep" is a military word; it means to "guard, to garrison, to fortify yourself," because you are under attack! You have to preserve that love of God that is in you, so you protect it, you build a wall, you edify yourself. Do not let anything destroy love with its forgiveness, patience and forbearance. Do not let that love be destroyed out of your life.

Some of you may be on the verge of doing that today. You may be in danger of that. Perhaps some of you have slipped; maybe you have lost some ground and feel you can no longer love that person because of the things that have happened. Keep yourself in the love of God!

And of some have compassion, making a difference...

Jude 22

This tells us that there are different ways to deal with different situations. A better translation would be: "upon some have compassion who waver and doubt." See, some of the people we're trying to help are double-minded. They are unstable souls and unstable personalities. We meet them one time and they flop this way, and the next time we meet them they flop the other way. Jude says when you're dealing with somebody like that, then you have to have *compassion*.

Be patient while you're seeking to bring them through, and by your witness, bring them into the ways of God.

> **And others save with fear, pulling them out of the fire;**
> **hating even the garment spotted by the flesh.**
> **Jude 23**

With some people you are going to have to be like the fire department. These people are in a building and it is on fire and about to be destroyed, and time is running out. You have to go and snatch them out of the peril they are in.

But there is another classification — the one where he says "hating even the garment spotted by the flesh." He says that some of the people you are trying to help are contaminated. They may have been soiled by sin, the sewers of sinfulness that they have been wallowing in for so long. He said that we have to be careful when we help these kind of people lest we be victimized and become what they are. We have to treat them like somebody who has a deadly contagious disease. You have to walk in wisdom, and in the counsel of God, if you're going to be any positive help to people like that.

Let me show you another verse. Turn to 2 Timothy 2:24.

> **And the servant of the Lord must not strive; but be**
> **gentle unto all men, apt to teach, patient...**

You have to be strong in order to help someone who is weak. If you have become unstable, then you have lost your influence. If you become like the other person who needs help, then you have removed yourself as an instrument of God from being able to help others. If you want to be God's servant, you cannot enter into strife, but you have to be gentle, ready to teach and patient.

> **In meekness instructing those that oppose themselves;**
> **if God peradventure will give them repentance to the**
> **acknowledging of the truth...**
>
> 2 Timothy 2:25

I like the translation here in the KJV: "those that *oppose* themselves." Some people are their own worst enemy. People who are headstrong in rebellion and going in the opposite direction to the ways for God, those people are defeating themselves. They are their own opponent. Like a football player who gets dazed and runs to the wrong end zone, that is the way some people are who oppose themselves.

Jude, in these short verses, has been showing us the road back for our loved ones and those for whom we are interceding. First of all they have to be brought to *repentance*. Every one of them is going to have to come to repentance. You cannot do that for another person. What you are trying to do through your prayers, warfare and love, is to bring them to repentance and the acknowledging of the truth. Second, they have to *acknowledge the truth:* concerning sin, concerning salvation, concerning the working of Satan. They have to accept the truth of God's word.

> **And that they may recover themselves out of the snare**
> **of the devil, who are taken captive by him at his will.**
>
> 2 Timothy 2:26

The third step here is *deliverance!* They have to be taken out of the power of the devil who has taken them captive, in a desire to bring them under his control and power.

So, these are the steps back for your loved ones:

1. **Repentance.**

2. **Acknowledgment of the Truth.**

3. **Deliverance out of the hand of the enemy.**

GUARD YOUR HEART, GUARD YOUR WALL

Let's go back to Nehemiah once more and study a few more verses. Nehemiah 4:7:

> But it came to pass, that when Sanballat, and Tobiah, and the Arabians, and the Ammonites, and the Ashdodites, heard that the walls of Jerusalem were made up, and that the breaches began to be stopped, then they were very wroth…

There you have it again. The reason they were mad was because the breaches and gaps in the wall were being closed, and the wall was being restored. Now saints, sometimes when those around us have breaches in their walls, it opens us up to have our walls torn down and have breaches made in our own walls. If we have not stayed true in love and forgiveness, then there can be breaches in our own walls. We need to pay attention to that. We can become so concentrated on what is happening to others that we may lose recognition of what the devil is able to gain in our own lives.

I want you to see both sides today. I want you to see now not only the needs your loved ones have, but I want you to see your own needs, and if perhaps breaches have been opened such that the enemy is able to get into your life. When the breaches get closed, the devil gets mad.

I like to frustrate the devil's plans for me. Amen? If I have a breach in my life, I want to repent of it, I want to forgive, and I want to receive God's forgiveness. I want that thing to be restored and built up so that I can live in peace and joy.

> And conspired all of them together to come and to fight against Jerusalem, and to hinder it.
>
> Neh. 4:8

As Jesus said in Matthew 12, Satan's kingdom is not divided. They are all working together. All these enemies conspire together to come and fight against Jerusalem and to hinder it. And the word *hinder*, in Hebrew, means to "injure, to confuse, and to cause to fail." That is what the enemy is trying to do.

> Nevertheless we made our prayer unto our God, and set a watch against them day and night, because of them.
>
> Neh. 4:9

We have to be vigilant in this battle. In our own personal battle mentioned before, there have been many times where we fought days on end. Sometimes I would be up in the night praying, and when I went to bed, then Ida Mae would get up. We had to have someone on the wall praying and interceding, only as led by the Lord.

BEWARE OF NEGATIVITY

> And Judah said, The strength of the bearers of burdens is decayed, and there is much rubbish; so that we are not able to build the wall.
>
> Neh. 4:10

These people of Judah were ready to give up, weren't they? They were saying, in essence,

"We can't bear the burden any longer, we might as well give up. Our strength has run out, and the task is too difficult. We did not now that there was so much rubbish. When we entered into this thing we had hope and anticipation that we could do this thing. But we cannot do it. We are not able; we have to give up; we can't finish it."

That attitude of hopelessness and despair can come upon us. I have to confess to you that a lot of times in this battle we've been in, I've been right there. I have said, "Oh no, this is just not turning out right." The devil tries to talk to me. You know, as much as I've been in spiritual warfare, as much as I have seen and observed the tactics of the devil, sometimes you can get tired. Sometimes your emotions can get so tired. Sometimes your physical body can get so tired. Perhaps you've lost sleep, and so many things have happened that you can fall into a weakened condition. So I am preaching to myself as I am preaching to you today. Let's not get into that weakened condition; let's realize who we are and who is on our side. Let's continue to press the battle until we see the victory of the Lord.

> **And our adversaries said, They shall not know, neither see, till we come in the midst among them, and slay them, and cause the work to cease.**
>
> Neh. 4:11

The moment that Judah made the bad confession, the devil says "Aha, aha! Now we can get them. They have their attention off the Lord; they have their attention off the building of the wall. They are thinking about themselves, and their own problems, and they are so aware of their own weakness. We can get them now."

The moment when we start making those negative confessions, and falling into doubt, is the opportunity the devil has been waiting for.

> And it came to pass, that when the Jews which dwelt
> by them came, they said unto us ten times, From all
> places whence ye shall return unto us they will be upon
> you.   Neh. 4:12

This was the kinfolk, their own people talking, who told them ten times that they could not finish the work, that the enemies were so strong that they would come in and defeat them. Have any of you had that problem with your kinfolk? Either your natural kinfolk or your spiritual kinfolk? Some of them have come in and told you to give up, that there is no hope. Imagine them coming to you and repeating it ten times as in Nehemiah!

YOUR FAMILY AS AN ARMY

Looking on, in verse 13, we read the following:

> Therefore set I in the lower places behind the wall, and
> on the higher places, I even set the people after their
> families with their swords, their spears, and their bows.

They were set up in family units to fight! Do you know that a family is a part of the army of God? Psalm 127:3–5 says,

> Lo, children are an heritage of the LORD: and the fruit
> of the womb is his reward.
>
> As arrows are in the hand of a mighty man; so are
> children of the youth.
>
> Happy is the man that hath his quiver full of them: they
> shall not be ashamed, but they shall speak with the
> enemies in the gate.

"They" shall subdue the enemy in his gates. Who will? The family will! Have you ever considered your family as part of the army of God? It is like a company of soldiers in God's army, and your family has the responsibility of defeating the enemy at his gates.

> **And I looked, and rose up, and said unto the nobles, and to the rulers, and to the rest of the people, Be not ye afraid of them: remember the LORD, which is great and terrible, and fight for your brethren, your sons, and your daughters, your wives, and your houses.**
>
> Neh. 4:14

What keeps us in the battle? Keeping our eyes on the Lord. Remember the Lord! Don't be afraid, but remember that the Lord is *great* and *terrible* in battle. And the Lord is on our side.

> **And it came to pass, when our enemies heard that it was known unto us, and God had brought their counsel to nought, that we returned all of us to the wall, every one unto his work.**
>
> Neh. 4:15

Hallelujah! So the work went on. As you read further in Nehemiah you find that the wall was built and the breaches were closed and the enemy was shut out. They won the victory over their adversaries!

CONCLUSION

Saints, we don't rush into deliverance or spiritual warfare, but we do so equipped with the Truth. It is first and foremost the Truth that sets us free.

We are going to learn the things that God wants us to learn so that will be ready. We are not only in a battling business, we are in a building business as well.

Nehemiah had to confront the enemy. God's people have had to fight, but the greatest purpose that we have is not just to fight but *to build*. To build the walls. There is no need to come against the enemy unless you build the wall. Because if you leave a breach in the wall then he has the opportunity to get back in.

Let's begin by paying attention to the breaches that are in our own lives, and give priority to that first. If there has been sin that has opened up a way of attack against you, if you need to ask God's forgiveness for what you've done, for your attitudes, for words that you've spoken and the actions that you taken, don't be too proud to repent and to ask the Lord to forgive you. If you have offended others or wounded others, ask them to forgive you. Get things right in your own heart. Don't harbor resentments or bitterness. Don't let any ill will fester in your heart. Close that breach because ill will is a breach for the enemy to enter your life.

With those steps, you will be in a stronger position to be used of God, and to bring your loved ones into the ways of God.

Now remember who you are, you are the army of God! Get the Word of God in your mouth and let it come out. Every weapon you have comes out from between your lips; that is where your weapons come from. Your weapons include the faith that you speak, the confession that you speak, the praise that comes out of your mouth, the Word of God that comes out of your mouth. It is the testimony of Jesus Christ that you profess. That is what defeats the enemy!

We are believing God to do some mighty things on the behalf of your loved ones! When you enter into this kind of intercession, it can be some of the most strenuous work that you can get involved in. This is not something that you perform in a casual way; you walk it out in the Spirit of God. You enter into battle and don't turn back. You say "Devil, I am going to stay in this fight and I am going to see this through, and we are going to have victory!"

You can't waver, and you can't doubt; you have to be willing to persist. Amen?

So once you start, you are going to follow the Lord, day and night. He will speak to you, and give you Scripture. He will give you *words of knowledge.* You will know what the enemy is going to do before he does it. You are going to know what God's counterattack is and you are going to be walking in the Spirit as God gives you victory. *Hallelujah!*

Talk to the devil. Bind his power off of your loved ones. Say this prayer with me:

PRAYER FOR
OUR LOST LOVED ONES

In the name of Jesus, I am a believer and not a doubter. God is true. God is the God of war. He is the God of battle. He has promised to help me. He has promised to fight for me. I align myself with God. I come against you demon spirits that attack my family, and my loved ones, I bind you in the name of Jesus.

You spirit of blindness that blinds my friends and my loved ones from seeing God and His truth, who blind them to the Gospel, we take authority over you and we stop you. We bind your power and forbid you to blind them any longer. You loose them now in the mighty name of Jesus.

I stand against the spirits of rebellion. I bind you in the name of Jesus. You loose my loved ones. They will be yielded to God's authority.

I come against the spirits of guilt, the spirits of condemnation, that tell them that God will not forgive. I loose my loved ones from the spirit of condemnation. I command you to let them go, in the name of Jesus.

Every demon that works against my friends and family, I assault the gates of hell and I bind your powers. I frustrate you. You tormenting and harassing spirits, I command the forces of the Lord of Hosts to torment and harass you; that the *tormentor* might instead become the *tormented*, the *persecutor* might instead be the *persecuted*. In the name of Jesus.

Now Lord God, I intercede on their behalf. Throw the enemy into confusion, let his plans be frustrated. Cut him off, that he cannot fulfill the plans he has devised.

Lord I repent of my own sins. I want to be used of you. I ask you to cleanse my heart, that I would not be a part of the problem. That I would be an instrument used of you to be a witness and a help in the lives of others. I receive your forgiveness.

I receive your strength. Lord give me your Spirit,

give me Your wisdom. Show me how to walk. Show me the workings of the enemy. I am not of darkness, I am of the light and I walk in the light. I walk in Your truth. I am not ignorant of Satan's devices.

We claim the victory, in the name of Jesus! We fight for our brothers, we fight for our sisters, we fight for our households, in the name of Jesus!

Thank you Lord for victory in Jesus' name.

Amen.

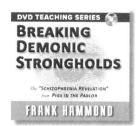

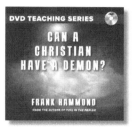

LEARN THE BLESSINGS OF GOOD SOUL-TIES & HOW TO BREAK UNGODLY TIES...

"Here at last is a thorough and theologically sound treatment of a little understood subject"   - from the Foreword by **Frank Hammond**

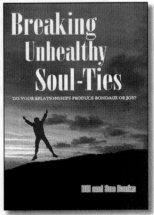

9780892281398

BREAKING UNHEALTHY SOUL-TIES
by Bill & Sue Banks

Today's world has conditioned us to give our soul to another without thought of the long-term consequences. Many are tired and weary from heartbreak, and from living under the power of the demonic. God desires to restore our souls that we might be able to seek Him with our whole spirit, soul and body. Unhealthy soul-ties seek to prevent this, through the control of one individual over another.

STUDY GUIDE:
BREAKING UNHEALTHY SOUL-TIES
BY BILL & SUE BANKS

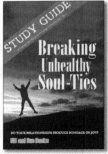

9780892282043

9780892284351

SOUL TIES

Frank Hammond's booklet on soul ties. Good soul ties include marriage, friendship, parent to child, and between sincere Christians. Bad soul ties include those formed from fornication, evil companions, perverted family ties, with the dead, and demonic ties through the Church.

AUDIO CD: FREEDOM FROM DEMONIC SOUL TIES

Frank Hammond teaches on healthy and unhealthy soul ties in this Audio series, including an extended ministry time at the end for breaking demonic ties to the soul.

9780892283613 CD

9780892280179

CONFRONTING FAMILIAR SPIRITS

A person can form a close relationship with an evil spirit, willfully or through ignorance, for the purposes of knowledge, financial gain, promotion or power. When a person forms a relationship with an unclean spirit, he or she "has a familiar spirit" or what can be called a "*spirit guide*." Familiar spirits operate as counterfeits to the gifts of the Holy Spirit. These counterfeit spirits are found throughout society, even at times within the Church. The Holy Spirit offers all we need in terms of access to the spiritual realm

9780892282036

OBSTACLES TO DELIVERANCE

WHY DELIVERANCE SOMETIMES FAILS

Why does deliverance sometimes fail? This is, in essence, the same question raised by Jesus' first disciples, when they were unable to cast out a spirit of epilepsy from a young child. Jesus gave a multi-part answer which leads us to take into account the strength of the spirit confronted and the strategy of warfare employed.

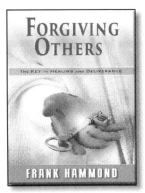

9780892280766

FORGIVING OTHERS:
THE KEY TO HEALING & DELIVERANCE

Unforgiveness is an obstacle to our walk with Jesus, and can be a roadblock to the deliverance and freedom of our souls. Frank Hammond explains the spiritual truths in the necessity of forgiveness and the blessings of freedom which result.

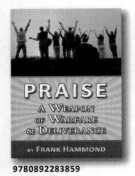

9780892283859

PRAISE: A WEAPON OF DELIVERANCE

Praise is a mighty weapon and the enemy knows it. He detests it because he fears it. Why? Because it is such a powerful force that destroys his grip on the spiritual atmosphere around us. *Praise clears the air*. What happened when David began to play on his harp and sing praise to his God? The evil spirit departed from King Saul. As you praise the Lord, things begin to happen in the unseen realm. A demon cannot exist in that atmosphere — he simply cannot function.

9780892281602

THE PERILS OF PASSIVITY

There is a purpose in God for each of us - and it is not passivity! Passivity is a foe to all believers in Christ – it can even hinder our intimacy with Jesus. Without an aggressive stance against the enemy, we can easily fall into passivity, and our service to the Lord can be limited. We lose our spiritual sharpness, which as Paul says, is necessary for us to be "sober, alert and diligent."

9780892281046

THE SAINTS AT WAR

There is a war on for your community, your city and your nation. Christians are in conflict with demons and territorial spirits. This is nothing new: the prophet Daniel confronted the "prince of Persia" when interceding for the captive people of God. Thanks to the power of the Holy Spirit, now you and I can be involved in this fight to change the course of history.

9780892280322

DELIVERANCE FROM FAT & EATING DISORDERS

Help for those who have been unable to lose weight or have struggled with eating disorders. Learn about possible spiritual roots and spiritual issues related to food. This is an eye-opening look at the role food can play as a substitute for stability in the love of Jesus. Bill Banks reveals dozens of spiritual reasons for unnatural weight gain, as well as eating disorders like Bulimia and Anorexia.